War Zones

Zvi A. Sesling

Nixes Mate Books
Allston, Massachusetts

Copyright © 2018 Zvi A. Sesling

Book design by d'Entremont
Cover photograph from the collection of Lauren Leja

All rights reserved. This book or any portion thereof may not be reproduced or used in any manner whatsoever without the express written permission of the publisher except for the use of brief quotations in a book review or scholarly journal.

Thank you to editor Susan J. Dechter.

Thank you to Publisher Michael McInnis for his hard work and patience.

ISBN 978-1-949279-01-6

Nixes Mate Books
POBox 1179
Allston, MA 02134
nixesmate.pub/books

For Those Who Serve Now
and
Those Who Served

I hate war as only a soldier who has lived it can, only as one who has seen its brutality, its stupidity.
– Dwight D. Eisenhower

Contents

Eleven Guys, USN, 1968	1
And The War Went On	7
Vietnam Memorial I	9
Inside The Head The War Rages On	10
Soldier In The Desert	12
What Armies Learn	13
Rice Paddy Dream	14
Soldiers	15
The Dead Refused Us	17
The Fallen	18
Thoughts On War	19
I Remember The Day	20
Vietnam Memorial II	22
Ghosts In The Wall	22
Dream of the Apocalyptic End	23
Kent State Photo	24
Iraq War	25
Memory of the Lost Soldier	26
You Emerge Victorious From	27
The Maze You Are Traveling In	27
What Is Peace	29

Hundred Years Wars	30
His Life Ended Under A Bridge	31
War I	32
War Zones	34
War Children	35
Vietnam Memorial III	36
Aftermath	37
War II	38
In The Desert	39
The Subject Is War	40
Red Desert	41
The Ex-Hippie	42
Boots On The Ground	45
Stage With No Backdrop	46
War Cries	47
War III	48
War IV	50
Explaining War	51
War Never Ends	53
Veterans Day	54
What They Did	55

War Zones

Eleven Guys, USN, 1968

Prologue

There was a war over there
somewhere most of us didn't know
about, especially those of us in Norfolk
where you were paid sixty-four bucks
every two weeks and you paid someone
other than yourself four dollars to
stand your watch in the middle of
of the night and they'd sleep on desks
where the cockroaches crawled

I

Commander Balls was the leader
he wanted to be at sea, he wanted
command of some destroyer lobbing
shells into some North Vietnamese shit hole
the unseen victims – the body count – all
parts count: 2 arms = 2 dead Cong
doesn't matter it's from the same body
or if the arms could only fit an infant
two down, a million to go: Balls is doing his job

2

And Crabbe, a low class first class petty officer
married to a whore in Sebu City, he shipped
back here, left her there, walked around singing
a variation of Sinatra's *Strangers in the Night*:
"Strangers in your wife, etc.", fat slob of a man yet
cheerful and carefree, didn't give a damn about much
except the strangers in his wife and her serving booze
at the base bar over there almost like handing a glass
to him who was looped each morning singing Sinatra

3

Who forgets "Mad Crad" conceited and with Texas
twang and better-than-thou-airs, a perfect square knot,
spit polished shoes and always ready to prove his
superiority over everyone, except the kid named Brody
whose uncle was an admiral – made him better too
Crad would disagree with everyone – he knew better –
and made it to PO3 and became ever more obnoxious
but he could write and do things the "Navy way" and
everyone believed he'd retire someday as a lifer

4

The sounds of Hank Williams singing
Your Cheating Heart
making noise like a tortured prisoner from Belieu's
tape recorder – O how we hated that tape
and we finally threw it in the ocean
where it sank like a Viet Cong
junk in the Gulf of Tonkin
with Hank's heart aboard, but Belieu, that
Macon cracker had another tape hidden and
two days later Hank was screeching at us
again, telling about cheating hearts, ours were
broken having to live with music that made
us hate country for years, maybe even lifetimes, which
is what it felt like being on that pier each day

5

Old Chief Harris walking around with his George
Wallace for President pin, telling Jews
they need to convert to Christianity
or rot in hell, he'd been in the Navy
so long he probably knew Jesus personally –
something he'd tell you was true because they talked
to each other each morning – didn't
know that Jesus was Jewish and

didn't believe it when told probably
has died by now and knows the
truth and would rather serve in hell
with Gen. Westmoreland and Robert McNamara
who joined the general so
the three of them and
ole George can try and figure out
what went wrong with the war
and with Jesus

6

If ever there was an alcoholic it was Stark,
drank each night and came in
hung over the next morning, booze odor
oozing out of the pores
like garbage from an overloaded
dumpster, the smell similar but Stark was mild
mannered and rarely
angry except when he was hung over – just
about every day, yet he could be more than fair
when he wanted, which wasn't quite as often
as when he was hung over and we never knew
why he was drinking: lost love, closet
homosexual, wanted to be an officer it was
anyone's guess what kept Stark on two feet
and the brain functioning – maybe he too
wanted to be over there yelling "Fire!"

7

The artist in the group was "Rembrant,"
cornstalk hick from somewhere in Iowa, but he
sure could draw cartoons and caricatures of anyone
on the pier, just give him pen and ink, a piece
of white hard stock and he'd draw you for a
fiver anyway you wanted: sportswriter, king,
admiral this hick with great talent and future – if
he ever left the Navy and found a place that
could utilize his talent – except New York is too
big and Iowa too small but somewhere he must
be drawing away making people ooh and aah
when he sketches them like some midway
cartoonist who will put you in a chair and draw
you for only $12.95.

8

There was Waters, married to a gal from the
Yukon, a simple and gentle man who said he'd
put in his twenty years for the pension so he
could support his wife and children and there
were two photogs, PO1 Coleman and PO3
Meane, a southerner who lived up to his name,
had a lousy personality and hated Jews gave
me one too many insults and when I nearly slugged

him Coleman bailed me out of a possible court marshal, a decent guy with a sense of fairness: the two of them good and bad on the same team because the military brings odd balls together like everyone and Lt. jg Petty, a Montana sad sack who couldn't make a decision and just wanted to get out

Epilogue

*So there we were the dozen of us
in Newport not telling the truth
about over there, not telling about
our warships being hit by rockets
from the shore, from the villages
that were reported wiped out, not
reporting our dead or wounded, not
reporting our failures and forever
unwilling to call it all a defeat*

And The War Went On

Kennedy is dead someone
shouted then we heard
Which one

So LBJ quit, Democrats chose
Humphrey who lost to
Nixon and the war went on
Kissinger was the most
important man in America
Nixon was reelected
Kissinger was even more
powerful and the war went on
and if we took the word of
our military leaders more than
the population of North Vietnam
had been killed we never admitted
we lost the war

At Kent State protesters who did not
want to die in the jungles of
Vietnam were shot dead by
National Guardsmen who probably
went to Vietnam and were shot
there, perhaps by friendly fire

and the war went on abandoned
by our allies, the news reported
what happened, never reported
we lost the war

Vietnam Memorial I
a memory

Descend into America's hell
black wall rising like death itself
sinking lower, depression pushing down
names, faceless names, staring back
through dotted i's and crossed t's
through curved c's and rounded o's
names staring back
letters rearrange and ask,
'Why am I here? Why not you?'

No answers
never were
just names and tears
from those who stare
at the names

Inside The Head The War Rages On

Morning jumps up like a baby
and you want to change the
diaper of your life, the woman
who has treated you like a
prisoner of war, the children who
hound as if you are in Baskersville
while the dog you should be
walking has done his thing in the
corner of the living room

Four flavors of depression
you choose vanilla which
happens to be the scent of the
candle the woman burned when
you found her in your bed with
someone from Harry's Bar & Grille

Longing for the peaceful days of
war in the jungle or desert when
in the heat you smell the enemy
miles away even when melted
into vines or rocks or when hiding
in caves and the odor of rotting corpses
that defied the separation of warrior
and civilian denied your senses

Some prefer sludge and toilets
to toiling among pieces of buddies blown
into granules of sand, who do not acknowledge
the greater good, who would sit like Napoleon
atop a steed at the pinnacle of battle and scratch
themselves while their minions died

Soldier In The Desert

The soldier in the desert is a poet.
He kills one day
He writes a poem the next
He sees the dead: flies landing like
   jet fighters on the red runways of the body
He writes about what he sees:
   a woman with scarf on head wailing,
   a child with scars on the face and on the heart
   a man without leg crawling home

He writes about soldiers as hunter and hunted
He writes about a suicide bomber scattered
across a hotel lobby mingled with guests and
workers

He sees the scorpion in his boot
He sees the bullet market for him screaming by
Luck
Sand in his nostrils

He pulls the trigger, and there is another death
Write
Kill
Write
Kill
The cycle continues in his dreams

What Armies Learn

Clouds come in like
wet gray army blankets
squeezing water until
grass grows a foot high
and trees drop their nuts
to float away like a Roman
fleet to Carthage

Weather and war are symbiotic.
Napoleon and Hitler learned
about Russian winters. America
did not survive Vietnamese
jungle rot

Parasitic vines grew in his ears,
the camouflage was real and
he will be found like a Machu
Pichu mummy in three hundred
or a thousand years, a marvel to
the victorious digger

Rice Paddy Dream

They were scorched and flesh
fell away, eye sockets
emptied, pelvis collapsed
bone white turned to ash
turned to wind that blew through
trees settled in rice paddies where
the enemy grew again to fight back

Soldiers

Soldiers With Guns
march to the heat of wailing

to the crunch of bones
to the solitude of graves

march in sand of ghosts
the rice paddies of memory

the cold of the past
the heat of today

the skies of tomorrow

Soldiers Without Guns
are forgotten by their women

stare through the bars of prison
lie in hospitals

hope for tomorrow
learn to pray

pray for another chance
plan escape routes

die for their country

The Dead Refused Us

The dead refused us first
Then the Army said *We want you*
The dead said *Join the Navy*
We didn't see the world
Or even America
Larry sat in San Diego
Typing names
I in Newport
The dead said *Good job*
You don't want to be here
With us
We thanked the dead
Served our time like prisoners
Following orders recording
The death of others

The Fallen

Glory is missing for him who bravely dies
  – Umberto Sava

In the soft earth of a distant jungle
the fallen soldier displaces
dust and leaf
found and buried
or
a flag draped casket
flown to home turf

In the sands of a foreign desert
where others risk lives to carry
the body to their base where
it is returned home to home earth
a news report gives a ten second memorial

Remembered or not he is already
forgotten by the nation
his moment of glory
he will not hear the cheers
for the returned living

Thoughts On War

Mother proudly sends her son off to war,
hopes he will be a hero   He comes

home in a casket, flag draped like a blanket.
mother becomes a protester, opposes war,

blames a president. Other mothers protest in
their hearts and still other mothers support the

cause or the death of a son would be meaningless.
War does not bring happiness to either side.

Soldiers die, civilians die. There are murders, rapes,
kidnappings, beheadings, suicide bombers, accidents,

friendly fire, and many wounded. War never ends, just
shifts battlefields, ensnares new people, encompasses

race, religion and politics. War is history.
War is ongoing.
War is the future.

I Remember The Day

I remember the day
The news reported a
plane hit one of
the towers, then
a second plane
then the Pentagon
the receptionist said,
*What's going on, it sounds
like we are under attack*
hours later we found
out her words were prophetic
war would begin again
America was at war
we would never be the same
politics degenerated
into near civil war
the economy tanked
U.S. auto companies failed
corporations cut jobs
moved overseas to maximize
profits while politicians
screamed for job creation and
allowed corporations to keep

laying off, kept sending work
out of the country and these
corporations demanded tax breaks
to create jobs taking the money and
laying off more workers while two
wars continued to sap the economy
two wars, a replay of the Crusades
in which horses are tanks, bow & arrow
have become missiles and wagons are
Hummers but soldiers are still human,
still die on battlefields, still lose limbs
eyes or lives

Vietnam Memorial II
Ghosts In The Wall

Ghosts are in the wall
behind the wall

looking out at you
you look at them

people touching names
reflections of sorrow

Ghosts speak to them
through names

Ghosts will last
through lifetimes

when people forget
Ghosts will not let them

Dream of the Apocalyptic End
(6 scenarios)

The Bomb is dropped
People look up, mouths open

. . .

The Bomb is dropped
People look up, scream

. . .

The Bomb is dropped
People run to basements

. . .

The Bomb is dropped
Children and animals cannot breathe

. . .

The Bomb is dropped
Vapor and dust rise

. . .

The Bomb is dropped
The dream ends

Kent State Photo

She is frozen in time
kneeling on one knee
arms spread
as if pleading
for life

The body lies
face down
in front of her
with no feeling
drained of life

Her face shows
agony of disbelief
that a soldier of her
country could kill a
fellow citizen

Iraq War

Boys just out of high school, the smell of the locker room still in their nostrils

Their girls at home like trained rabbits

Lunch grimed with sand, water as important as bullets

The flak jacket their brick wall of protection as they patrol streets as narrow as a finger, as long as a prayer

The fireplace at home not as hot as the hell they are in

Memory of the Lost Soldier

Khe San or Baghdad or Kabul
he is not forgotten – still alive they think
someone remembers he was shipped home
but never got there
lost perhaps on the way
or at arrival – maybe Rome or Paris or London
perhaps New York or Los Angeles
big enough to be lost
with drugs or without
with alcohol or without
finding a bed with a woman or without
finding warmth with a fire or without
finding something to keep him going
or not

You Emerge Victorious From The Maze You Are Traveling In
– for a friend with PTSD

Like a secret garden behind a Victorian home
Lost among bushes and trees
Turning a corner only to find more corners
Paths leading to dead ends

People passing with blank faces
Empty stares of yearning
Or hands feeling ahead as if
The follower is blind or in the dark

Pathways of pebbles give hope
Yet lead nowhere except deeper into
The hidden world of lost rabbits and mice
Where no bird alights

Groping for a leaf with no meaning, no direction
A branch points the way out
Is it forgotten reality
Or is it subterfuge

An end with no meaning
A meaning with no end

Like a book with no pages
A song with no sound

Up ahead there is an opening
Beyond the opening an exit
You emerge victorious from the
Maze you are traveling in

What Is Peace

What is peace
        silent guns
           barbed wire fences
          soldiers patrolling

Is there music in the background
Is the colonel shaving
Is supper being served

Are lovers holding hands

Do eyes watch everyone

Is there an end to it all

Does peace unite

Hundred Years War

Heard the lament of Flanders Field
saw the flag atop Suribachi
landed at Inchon
counted body parts at Khe San
wiped feet in the sands of Kuwait City
again in Baghdad and Kabul
fired at the hordes
who learned from us to hide behind
rocks and walls and wear camouflage
to be where they ain't
disappear in the desert like a sand beetle
kill because someone says
to free their country

His Life Ended Under A Bridge

His life ended under a bridge
near Pittsburgh
a high school football hero
who joined the army
went to Nam
killed and was nearly killed
found solace in drugs
returned home
found a woman with drugs
who hung out under bridges
until one day
during an argument
she shot him in the head
his own pistol from a war
in which he died twice

War I

I was serving at home
yet war changed all
our lives

Many came back with drugs
but without their arms or legs
angry as rabid dogs or pumpkins without smiles

Some prefer to dig in
sludge and toilets to toiling among pieces
of buddies blown into granules of sand

Nor do they sit atop a white steed at the pinnacle
of battle like Napoleon scratching
themselves while their pawns died

Politicians, presidents, money hungry
who see profit in war
defeat or victory is totaled by profit not territorial gain

Oil companies, weapons manufacturers, vehicle makers
stock brokers and hedge fund managers
see wealth increase all march to the green tune

Stocks rise as green bills fill pockets and portfolios
Democrats, Republicans, manufacturers
industrialists, there is money to be made from war

While others who hoped to escape poverty
have their blood flowing red in deserts or jungles
their red becoming the profit makers' green
while a generation of the future lies underground

War Zones

Jet fighters fly overhead on their
way to a picnic of roast innocents

Mud huts in the desert have no
air conditioning and people bake

Cannibals have a feast
when they leave their jungle mansions

Cows burp grass into the faces of
their killers before becoming dinner

Fish sacrifice themselves to the worm
of the endless fry pan

Vegetables cry when severed from
their roots

Flowers seek revenge following
their amputation from life

And the innocents wail at the loss
of everything as the sound of jets fade

War Children

Flat daddy: cardboard cutouts,
something to remind the two
year-old who his father is

No legs. No playing baseball
with his children. He can stand
and hit, but he can't run

No arms. The sons wants baseball
he wants soccer. Why? He has no
answer

Another child watches a friend play
with daddy. The child has no daddy.
The child only remembers a casket

Children are wounded. For the child
whose father is dead, something has
been snuffed

For the children of war, even when a
parent returns, there is so much pain

Vietnam Memorial III

The Vietnam Memorial of Maya Lin
is a giant mirror where the living and
the dead seem to intermingle
   – *Murray Dewart*

Whose face do you see – son
or brother crying as you are

Sorrow on a day of sunshine
that cannot warm the heart

The name reminds he is a
son or brother gone forever

The face in the mirror is there
and though the heart breaks

Both leave with an imperceptible
smile at having seen the departed

Note: The epigraph by sculptor Murray Dewart is found on Page 21 in his Introduction of *Poems About Sculpture*, in "Everyman's Library Pocket Poets"

Aftermath

wives divorced them
lovers abandoned them
children forgot them
lost their families
police arrested them
they sank into homelessness

what they knew was forgotten
what they learned was drugs
shop lifting or begging
burglary or armed robbery
anger and drugs, drugs and murder
they learned about death

War II

Send our leaders to war instead of our youth
        let them carry the guns
        let them drop the bombs
        diffuse the bombs
Tell them they must die for their country
        for the good
        for someone else
Let them lose an arm or both
        a leg or both
        an ear or both
Maybe that will stop war
        our leaders do not want to die
        they let others go to their graves
        so they can live

In The Desert

Hot winds blow bullets through air,
sand grains explode.

A soldier loses two legs.
A soldier loses two arms.
A soldier loses two eyes.
A soldier loses his head.
A soldier loses his heart.

Body parts of the enemy are counted:
One leg, one dead.
One arm, one dead.

The soldier with no legs, the soldier
with no arms, the soldier with no eyes
are alive.

One wishes for life.
One wishes for death.
One wishes for his mother.

War takes much, gives little.
The sands turn red, cities bleed.
Victory never seems near.

The Subject Is War

There are soldiers in Afghanistan
There are soldiers in Iraq
Soldiers are dying in Afghanistan
Soldiers are dying in Iraq

At home crippled soldiers rehab
At home new soldiers prepare for battle
At home politicians defend their war
At home politicians are blamed for opposing the war

Debate after debate politicians try to score points
The soldiers are forgotten
Politicians are debating
Soldiers are dying

Red Desert

Blood runs across the desert
like a snake with no tongue

Bones bleach like a Georgia O'Keefe
painting and tanks rumble forward

There are no trees to hide behind
no shelter from airborne bombs

Blood is the oasis of war
the red sun descends on the red desert

A parched tongue, a grasping hand crawls
heat and blood make the desert red

The Ex-Hippie

Some doped up ex-hippie
living on the street
a tin cup (made in China)
bought in the dollar store
and you wonder how they
ever let him in the front door

He's sitting here at the corner of
Congress & Franklin streets smoking
a toke as cops walk by and know it's
a bigger pain in the ass to arrest him than
to leave him there in his camouflage
hat and t-shirt

Every once in a while someone drops
a nickel or penny in the tin cup and he
nods as dilated pupils squint in daylight
food dredged from a dumpster in his beard
shoes with holes and the t-shirt has
a peace sign

For a buck he'll tell you he skipped
Vietnam for a ticket to Canada worked
on a farm for his drugs (grew some of

his own) and came back with a different
name left a couple kids up there
by two women

A Vietnam vet once kicked the tin cup
scattering the change because he
didn't like the ex-hippie's t-shirt
camouflage outfit or the ex-hippie
though the vet had survived war drugs
and his own demons

The vet is a business man now in suit
and tie drives a Caddy Escalade has
a wife and three children one in graduate
school one in college one in high school
house in the suburbs two dogs cat
talking parrot

Sometime the ex-hippie wanders
the streets like a lost cow at midnight
wanders out to the suburbs where
he pisses on the businessman's lawn
an act of defiance an infiltration of
the military-industrial elite

One winter he was found frozen dead
the rolled marijuana stick still in his hand
the beard a horror of icicles
missed in a police roundup of the
homeless and suddenly child appears
misses the funeral then sues the city

Boots On The Ground

Not John or Joe or Mack
Just boots on the ground
Not 18-year olds or 20-year olds
Not Corporals or Lieutenants
Instead laced up boots filling with sand
Boots don't matter because they are not people
No faces of those in the boots
The ones who send the boots to combat
Never see the boots, never see the faces
Never see tears or flags on coffins

Stage With No Backdrop

Soldier in camouflage uniform
Weapon in hand

Iraq, Afghanistan, Israel, Sri Lanka, Congo,
Pakistan, Ethiopia, Chechnya, Somalia

Many countries, many soldiers
Dead, they all look the same
Crying mothers, defeated fathers

War Cries

War used to be honorable, patriotic
you signed up (or were drafted) to
defend your country, the uniform
was a proud flag, like a policeman
or firefighter – you were going to keep
the bad guys from getting us

Then came Vietnam which began
honorably but degenerated into a
morass of drugs, death and demoralized
soldiers

Grenada was quick and glorious as we
swept over a small Cuban contingent the
way the Sioux must have thundered over
Custer

Kosovo was a simple "just" excursion to
prevent genocide, but then came 9/11
American forces entered Afghanistan
and Iraq and now America is not considered
"good guys" as locals find us no different from
those considered "bad guys"

War III

The leader sits back in a comfortable
chair. Perhaps one sat in so often it sags

like the leader's chin, which is held up
by his right hand, the hand which will

soon sign a paper sending more soldiers
to war, more young men to die for their

country, for their leader's resolve to win,
for the victory the leader has promised.

At the same time a terrorist leader sends
young boys to blow themselves up and

with them a bus, a car, a restaurant, a store
where tourists are purchasing souvenirs

Young boys who will never know
love, marriage or their own children

These boys know only the hate they have been taught.
War is always somewhere and someone is always dying.
The war room has no windows

to view debates over
        acceptable casualties

President's office curtains pulled
shut so no one hears about
        troop surges

Venetian blinds in congress closed
to avoid people seeing arguments
over money needed for war

Tomorrow another casket
delivered to parents whose eyes
        never dry

War IV

A bomb explodes in a car – 80 dead
A suicide bomber in a bus – 62 dead
A drone blows up a car – 5 dead
A rocket explodes in a field – 2 dead
A rocket hits a city – 16 dead
A soldier fires into a crowd – 3 dead

War doesn't play a nice game
War plays death, and age is not a factor

Three-year-olds on both sides die
as easily as 20-year-old soldiers
as easily as a grandfather at age 80
as easily as a gun or rocket fired

Explaining War

First find a clown with fuzzy hair, big
painted mouth and beady eyes to get
everyone's attention, especially the children

Lead an elephant with the right hand
and a donkey with the left and women
in trapeze or cheerleader outfits

Then come the senators in purple robes
and finally the president in his emperor's
suit and crown

Let them explain why one political party
starts a war and the other party objects until
the objectors become the majority

Let them pile the money spent on the wars
higher than the tallest building, wider than
the widest river

Let the clowns, elephants, donkeys, congressmen
senators and president explain why the young,
a son or brother is dead, why a parent must die

War is in a distant desert or jungle that children in school have not even studied and will never see unless the wars go on, endless wars led by clowns

War Never Ends

War never ends
Guns do not stop

Bombing does not halt
An ambush or mines happen

Faces resemble enemy
Or dead comrades

At night dead return to haunt
A horror movie of peeling faces

Dreams never end
Dead never leave

Skin raw and eyes hollow
Bones in pieces and minds shattered

Soldiers cannot forget
Nor can they sleep

Veterans Day

He stands before the mirror
of self-contempt

His toes dangle over the
precipice of self-destruction

Memories flash back like
an M-16 in the dark jungle

Cannon fire in night desert
recoil dulling his brain

How could it have all been
with him the unwilling actor

What They Did

*Ask Not What your country
can do for you, ask what you
can do for your country*
– Pres. John F. Kennedy, Inauguration Speech, January 20, 1961

So they listened to him, first they
went off to combat poverty, ignorance, illness
earned little, suffered for their country

Others fought the communist threat in the
jungles and died for their country, thousands dead,
thousands wounded, maimed, psychologically damaged

Then another war, thousands
more dead and wounded – lost arms, legs, faces
they knew why they were there – doing it for their country

How much more can the young be asked to do?
How many presidents ask them to serve their country?
How many young will not ask, but will die trying to do?

Acknowledgments

Some of these poems may have been published in slightly different forms in the following publications: *Nixes Mate Review, Slant, South Boston Literary Gazette, Stone Soup, The Tower (Canada), Proud To Be: Writing By American Warriors, Vol. 4*

About the Author

Zvi A. Sesling is the Poet Laureate of Brookline, MA and a prize winning poet. He has been published widely in print and online nationally and internationally. Sesling is Editor of *Muddy River Poetry Review*, publishes *Muddy River Books* and reviews for the *Boston Small Press and Poetry Scene*. He has been a featured reader in various venues in the Boston area and San Diego, as well as on local cable television and radio stations. Sesling has been a featured reader at the Boston National Poetry Festival and the Massachusetts Poetry Festival. His poems have been featured at the Spring Rain Festival on the island of Cyprus, and the Somerville, MA "Arts at the Armory". Sesling has been nominated four times for a Pushcart Prize and was awarded First Prize in the Rueben Rose International Poetry Competition. He is author of three volumes of poetry, *The Lynching of Leo Frank* (Big Table Publishing Co, 2017), *Fire Tongue* (Červena Barva Press, 2016), and *King of the Jungle,* (Ibbetson St. Press, 2010) as well as two chapbooks *Love Poems From Hell* (Flutter Press, 2017) and *Across Stones of Bad Dreams* (Červena Barva Press, 2011). He has taught at Suffolk University, Emerson College and Boston University. He lives in Brookline MA with his wife Susan J. Dechter.

42° 19' 47.9" N   70° 56' 43.9" W

Nixes Mate is a navigational hazard in Boston Harbor used during the colonial period to gibbet and hang pirates and mutineers.

Nixes Mate Books features small-batch artisanal literature, created by writers who use all 26 letters of the alphabet and then some, honing their craft the time-honored way: one line at a time.

nixesmate.pub/books

www.ingramcontent.com/pod-product-compliance
Lightning Source LLC
Chambersburg PA
CBHW071756080526
44588CB00013B/2261